P9-CFI-854

INSECTS &
SPIDERS

SOCIAL INSECTS

Jonathan Sutherland

GARETH**STEVENS**
PUBLISHING
A Member of the WRC Media Family of Companies

Please visit our Web site at: **www.garethstevens.com**
For a free color catalog describing Gareth Stevens Publishing's
list of high-quality books and multimedia programs,
call 1-800-542-2595 (USA) or 1-800-387-3178 (Canada).
Gareth Stevens Publishing's fax: (414) 332-3567.

Library of Congress Cataloging-in-Publication Data

Sutherland, Jonathan, 1958-
    Social insects / Jonathan Sutherland.
       p. cm. — (Nature's monsters. Insects & spiders)
    Includes bibliographical references and index.
    ISBN-10: 0-8368-6851-X — ISBN-13: 978-0-8368-6851-7 (lib. bdg.)
    1. Insects—Juvenile literature. 2. Insect societies—Juvenile literature. I. Title. II. Series.
QL467.2.S8755   2006
595.7156—dc22
                                         2006042361

This North American edition first published in 2007 by
Gareth Stevens Publishing
A Member of the WRC Media Family of Companies
330 West Olive Street, Suite 100
Milwaukee, WI 53212 USA

Original edition and illustrations copyright © 2006 by International Masters Publishers AB.
Produced by Amber Books Ltd., Bradley's Close, 74–77 White Lion Street, London N1 9PF, U.K.

Project editor: Michael Spilling
Design: Joe Conneally

Gareth Stevens editorial direction: Valerie J. Weber
Gareth Stevens editor: Leifa Butrick
Gareth Stevens art direction: Tammy West
Gareth Stevens production: Jessica Morris

Printed in the United States of America

1 2 3 4 5 6 7 8 9 10 09 08 07 06

Contents

Continents of the World

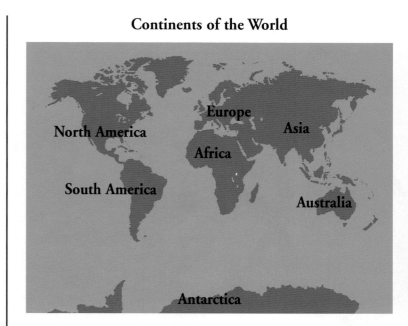

The world is divided into seven continents — North America, South America, Europe, Africa, Asia, Australia, and Antarctica. On the following pages, the area where each animal lives is shown in red, while all land is shown in green.

Words that appear in the glossary are printed in **boldface** type the first time they occur in the text.

Asian Long-Horned Beetle

The beetle folds up its wings under hard **wing cases** when it is not using them to fly.

Each leg ends in a claw that can grip almost any surface.

Its **mouthparts** are very tough and can chew easily through wood and bark.

The long-horned beetle's legs are covered with hairs that pick up **vibrations** in the air.

Before they become adult insects, Asian long-horned beetles are legless, wriggling **grubs.** These grubs live in tree wood. They **burrow** so many long tunnels into the tree trunks that the trees die.

Actual Size

Did You Know?

In the United States, Asian long-horned beetles have killed more than sixteen thousand trees in New Jersey alone. In the 1970s, long-horned beetles killed whole **plantations** in Southeast Asia.

2 In time, the grubs turn into adult beetles. The beetles chew their way through the wood, leaving holes and small piles of sawdust that show where they have been.

1 This man loading cargo onto a boat does not know that the crate contains some long-horned beetle grubs. The grubs survive in the wooden packing crate.

Where in the World

Asian long-horned beetles come from Japan, Korea, and China. They have also traveled across land to Europe and on cargo ships to the Americas, where they have thrived to become a major pest.

3 The cargo box is unloaded at a foreign port, and the adult beetles fly off to make a home in nearby trees.

Sand Wasp

The wasp has large eyes for spotting its prey.

The sand wasp has a tiny waist that allows it to turn around inside its many nests.

Hairs on the wasp's legs help it move sand and earth.

The wasp has two powerful jaws, which it uses for digging and carrying.

Sand wasps like to eat large, fat caterpillars. Some caterpillars are so heavy that the wasps have to drag them back to their nests. Sand wasps can drag caterpillars up to ten times their own weight.

Actual Size

1 A female sand wasp finds a large and juicy caterpillar. She **paralyzes** it with nerve **toxin**. The wasp then turns the caterpillar over and drags it toward her nest, holding it by its head.

2 The wasp pulls the caterpillar into the burrow and lays eggs on its body. She then seals up the entrance to the burrow.

3 When the eggs hatch, the **larvae** begin eating the caterpillar alive. The toxin helps stop the caterpillar from rotting. The mother will bring more caterpillars later.

Where in the World

Sand wasps can be found in Africa, Asia, Australia, Europe, and North and Central America. They favor dry earth or sand to make their burrows.

Cuckoo Wasp

The cuckoo wasp's **exoskeleton** is a strong, protective, armored coat covering its upper body.

The wasp's wings are powerful and beat so fast that people cannot see them. They give the insect tremendous speed.

Its **abdomen** is flexible and allows the wasp to tuck in its legs and curl up into a ball.

The stingless cuckoo wasp steals the nests of other wasps and bees. It plants its larvae there to feed on the **pupae** of the other insects.

1 The adult female hunts for a place to lay her eggs. She finds the empty clay nest of a **potter wasp**. She crawls into the entrance, but a potter wasp spots her. The potter wasp attacks to drive her away.

2 The cuckoo wasp curls up and produces a foul smell. The sting of the potter wasp cannot get through the cuckoo wasp's strong coat. The potter wasp rolls the cuckoo wasp out of its nest. The cuckoo wasp flies away unhurt.

African Driver Ant

The **soldier** driver ant's body is small compared to the much larger queen. She can produce two million eggs a month.

The large head of the soldier driver ant supports its heavy **mandibles**.

Its legs are jointed, and clawed feet help the ant move around easily.

The soldier ant's mandibles are huge and have sharp, cutting edges.

Every day, swarms of driver ants go out hunting for food. Soldier ants lead the way, followed by **worker** ants. The ants overwhelm everything in their path.

1 The worker ants rapidly overpower a locust and carry their **prey** back to their nest. Soldier driver ants do not rely on stings to attack. They use their large and powerful mandibles to create puncture wounds and tear off sections of their prey.

2 After stripping an area of food, the driver ants are forced to migrate to find new feeding grounds. The worker ants make temporary nests from living ants to house the queen.

Did You Know?

Swarms of driver ants take three minutes to travel 3 feet (1 meter).

The driver ant's nest is a maze of chambers and tunnels 13 feet (4 m) long. Up to twenty million worker ants live in one nest.

Where in the World

Driver ants live in the humid parts of Africa. Some **rain forests** contain more than 1.2 billion driver ants per square half mile (0.5 billion per square kilometer).

Army Ant

The army ant's eyes are so tiny that it can tell only whether it is day or night.

The army ant's long legs help it to move fast across difficult ground.

Its **antennae** are highly sensitive and follow trails laid by other ants.

The army ant has huge jaws to defend the colony from attackers.

Army ants can overpower animals much larger than themselves, even **scorpions**. They are highly social and live in a vast, **nomadic colony** with only one **breeding** queen.

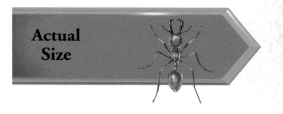

Actual Size

1 Army ants move in a long column. The worker ants carry the young while the soldiers guard the edge of the column. The younger ants form ladders over gaps in the forest floor.

2 The column will travel 656 feet (200 m) into the forest to set up a new camp. The queen joins them during the night. She then starts laying eggs. As many as 300,000 new adults will emerge before the ants move again after fifteen days.

Where in the World

The army ant can be found from Mexico south through Central and South America to northern Argentina. The army ant's **habitat** is **tropical** rain forests. In these forests, it can find a lot of prey.

Weaver Ant

A weaver ant's abdomen divides into two parts. A strong waist separates these parts. The rear part holds its stomach and intestine.

The weaver ant uses its eyes to understand signals from other ants in its colony.

Its powerful claws help it climb and grip leaves.

Its mandibles are sharp and strong. It uses them for building nests and fighting.

Weaver ants use scents and **body language** to communicate at least fifteen different messages to each other. They lay scent trails to show where food is and give out alarm signals when they are attacked.

Size

x2

1 Weaver ants build their nests in trees. Their nests are well hidden to protect them from **predators** and the weather. Weaver ants' nests are among the most complex of ant nests.

2 The ants use living leaves to build nests. First the ants make a chain of ant bodies from one leaf to the next. Then they shorten the chain, one ant at a time, until the leaf edges connect.

3 Once the edges are together, one ant holds a larva in its mandibles and squeezes it to produce silk. It uses the silk to glue the leaf edges together.

Where in the World

Weaver ants live in tropical climates, particularly in forests and valleys. They can be found in Africa, southern Asia, and in some parts of Australia.

Bullet Ant

The bullet ant's body is made up of ten different parts. The last three pieces contain its stinger.

The ant has eight **sensors** on its stinger that give it information about its prey.

The ant's antennae are designed to pick up warning chemicals from other worker bullet ants.

Its jaws are powerful pincers. These pincers are so sensitive that they can carry droplets of nectar.

The bullet ant's stinger is also an egg-laying tube. Only 0.11 inches (3 millimeters) long, the stinger holds two blades, each with ten saw-toothed **barbs**. Eleven muscles work the stinger.

1 Worker ants use their jaws to capture and kill small insects and grubs. If its prey struggles, the bullet ant uses its stinger.

2 Part of the bullet ant's stinger lies within its abdomen. A sac containing **venom** is attached to the stinger. The ant can also release a scent to call for help from other worker ants.

3 The legs of a bullet ant are very strong so it can run quickly. If a man could run as fast for his size as an ant can, he would be as fast as a racehorse.

Actual Size

Where in the World

Bullet ants can be found in the tropical areas of Central and South America, from Nicaragua to the Amazon Basin. They build their nests under trees in wet rain forests.

Bee-Killer Wasp

The bee-killer wasp's **compound** eyes let it see its surroundings very clearly.

It uses its antennae for detecting vibrations and for tasting.

The wasp uses its powerful mandibles to make tunnels and complex burrows.

Its stinger is a sharp, hollow tube that pumps venom into the honeybee.

Female bee-killer wasps attack honeybees. They force them to the ground and then paralyze them. The wasps carry their victims to their underground chambers as fresh, live food for their grubs.

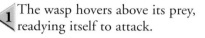

1 The wasp hovers above its prey, readying itself to attack.

2 The wasp grabs its prey with its long legs, avoiding the bee's deadly sting. The two enemies struggle, each trying to overpower the other.

3 The wasp seizes its chance and stings the bee. It squeezes the bee's abdomen to suck up the nectar. The helpless bee is paralyzed.

Actual Size

Did You Know?

As well as sucking up nectar, bee-killer wasps also suck the blood from their victims' wounds.

The bee-killer wasp not only hunts honeybees — its larvae also eat a wide range of other insects.

Where in the World

This wasp can be found wherever there are many bees. It is common in most parts of western, southern, and central Europe.

19

Harvester Ant

The ant's abdomen has a barbed stinger on its tip.

The ant's head is large, square, and covered with hair. It uses its head to sense movement.

The harvester ant's antennae are club shaped and sensitive to smell, taste, and touch.

Its jaws are designed to open seed husks and to attack enemies.

Harvester ants live in large mounds on dry plains and grasslands. They have barbed stingers that can harm larger animals, especially young animals such as calves.

1 A calf investigates a harvester ant mound in a field. Worker ants on the surface signal more ants to come to protect the colony. The workers stream out of the nest to attack the calf.

2 Ants swarm all over the calf and dig their powerful jaws into its skin. They pierce the animal with their barbed stingers. The calf is in great pain and collapses. It is paralyzed by the venom and soon dies.

Size

x2

Where in the World

There are twenty-two species of this ant in the southern and western United States. The Texan harvester ant is the most common. The Florida harvester ant is found east of the Mississippi River.

21

Slave-Making Ant

The slave-making ant's abdomen contains most of its most important organs.

Its eyes can pick out the outlines of large objects and the position of the Sun.

The ant uses its sharp jaws to cut chunks from its prey.

It uses its antennae to follow the scent trails left by other slave-making ants.

Slave-making ants get their name from stealing the **cocoons** of other ants. They carry them back to their own nest to use as future slaves for their colony.

1 Here, a pair of slave-making ants watch worker ants from a wood ant colony. They have followed the workers back to the nest. The slave-making ants return to their own home to lead their soldier ants to the wood ants' nest.

Size

x4

Did You Know?

Often, a slave-making colony produces more than one queen. When this happens, the younger queen will kill the existing queen and take her place. She then lays her eggs and is adopted by the colony.

2 The slave-making ants' army follows a scent trail and storms the wood ants' mound. They kill any of the ants that resist by biting into their abdomens or heads. They then steal the wood ants' cocoons.

Where in the World

There are five **species** of this ant. They can be found in parts of North America, Europe, Japan, and parts of Asia. They need to be close to other ant colonies.

Cicada Killer Wasp

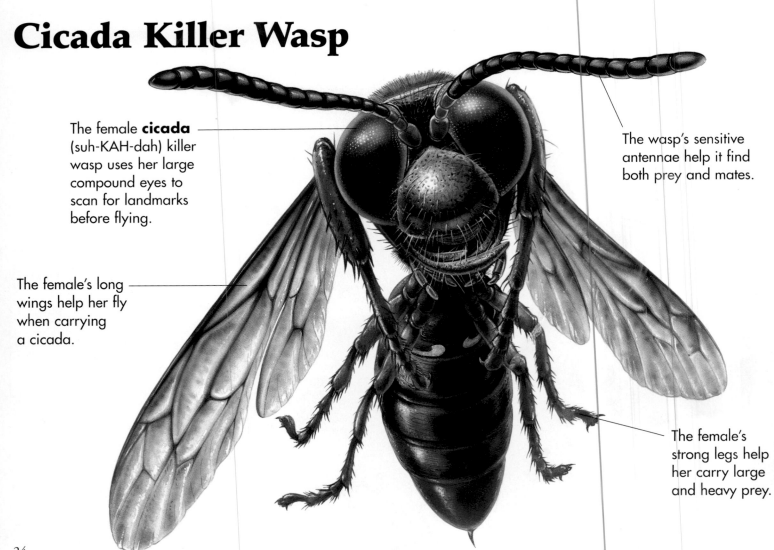

The female **cicada** (suh-KAH-dah) killer wasp uses her large compound eyes to scan for landmarks before flying.

The wasp's sensitive antennae help it find both prey and mates.

The female's long wings help her fly when carrying a cicada.

The female's strong legs help her carry large and heavy prey.

The female cicada killer wasp is an expert cicada hunter. She searches tree trunks and the lower limbs of trees for her prey.

The cicada killer wasp larva can grow to full size in five days. Male eggs are laid on a single cicada, but female eggs are given two or sometimes three cicadas because the female wasp is twice as large as the male and must have more food.

2 The wasp carries the cicada back to her burrow, grasping it with her hooked middle legs.

1 When the female spots a cicada, she pounces on it and clings as tightly as possible. She jabs a stinger into the cicada, paralyzing her prey in less than a minute.

3 The female drags the paralyzed cicada down into a cell and lays an egg inside the cell with the insect. She then seals the cell, and her larva feeds on the soft insides of the cicada.

Where in the World

This insect is most common in eastern North America. It chooses loose or sandy soil close to groups of cicadas. Gardens and other sunny habitats are ideal for their burrows.

Giraffe Beetle

The giraffe beetle's neck has a hinge like a desk lamp that allows its head to move up and down.

The giraffe beetle's long neck and head make up half its height.

The giraffe beetle has poor eyesight and can only see the movement of things and animals that are close by.

It uses its feelers to explore its surroundings and to pick up odors.

A male giraffe beetle's head is much longer than a female beetle's head. The length of its head is useful for attracting a mate. Male beetles with the longest heads scare off competing males with shorter heads.

1 Male giraffe beetles bob their heads up and down when competing to **mate** with a female. The ones with the shorter heads go away, leaving the tallest male to mate with the females.

Using her jaws and front legs, a female giraffe beetle rolls up **2** each of her eggs inside a leaf. If her head was as long as a male beetle's, she would not be able to do this.

3 The larva of the giraffe beetle grows safely inside its leaf nest. It uses parts of the leaf nest for food.

27

Common Wasp

The common wasp's two pairs of wings let it hover and change direction.

The wasp uses its antennae to communicate with other wasps.

Its jaws are powerful and allow it to chew its prey.

The yellow and brown stripes on a wasp's body warn predators to stay away.

28

Wasp love ripe fruit and sugary food and are a danger to picnickers. If someone swallows a wasp and it stings his or her throat or tongue, that person could die.

1 A wasp is attracted by the sugary smell of a soda. It lands on the can and goes inside, where it is trapped.

2 Unaware of the wasp, the girl drinks from the can. The wasp floats into her mouth. Trying to defend itself, it stings the back of her tongue.

3 The venom makes the girl's tongue swell. She could **suffocate**. She needs to get medical care right away.

Actual Size

Did You Know?

Male wasps do little except wait to mate with young queen wasps.

Any wasp grubs that die in the nest are eaten by other grubs.

Where in the World

In the past, the common wasp lived only in Europe. It has now spread across North and Central America, Asia, and Australia. In warmer countries, the wasps' colonies do not die in winter. They get bigger.

Glossary

abdomen — the lower section of an insect's body

antennae — a pair of feelers on an insect's head

barbs — sharp pointed objects pointing backward, like arrows or fish hooks

body language — body movements that send a message to another animal or person

breeding — producing young

burrow — to dig holes made in the ground by animals for shelter and protection; also the hole itself.

cicada — a large winged insect. The males buzz loudly.

citrus — fruit of the citrus family, including oranges, lemons, and grapefruit

cocoons — sacs, pouches, or cases that help protect the larvae before they change into adults

colony — ants that make up a single group around a queen

compound — made up of many parts

exoskeleton — a tough skeleton on the outside of an animal's body

fossils — the remains of a plant or animal that have been preserved in the earth or in a rock

grubs — another name for larvae

habitat — a place where an animal lives

larvae — the wormlike forms of many insects when newly hatched from an egg

mandibles — a pair of pincerlike jaws used by insects to cut up food

mate — to join together to produce babies

mouthparts — the parts of an insect used for feeding

nectar — a sweet liquid found in flowers

nomadic — moving from place to place with no fixed home

paralyzes — makes an animal unable to move

plantations — huge farms planted in just a few crops

potter wasp — wasps that form nests made of mud

predators — animals that hunt, kill, and eat other animals

prey — a creature hunted and killed for food

pupae — the stage between insect larvae and adults

rain forest — thick forest where lots of rain falls

rheumatism — stiffness or swelling in the muscles or joints

sensors — parts of an animal's body that can feel or sense

scorpions — members of the spider family with jointed bodies and poisonous stingers

soldier — referring to a person or animal who fights in war

species — groups of living things of the same type

suffocate — to cause an animal or person to stop breathing

toxic — poisonous

toxin — poisonous substance

tropical — referring to the warmest regions of the world, with lush plant life and lots of rain

venom — a poison made by an animal

vibrations — tiny motions caused by sounds or movements

wing cases — hard coverings that protect an insect's delicate flying wings

worker — referring to a person or animal who carries out tasks

For More Information

Books

About Insects. A Guide for Children (series).
   Cathryn Sill (Peachtree)

American Insects: A Handbook of the Insects of America North of Mexico. Ross Arnett (CRC Press)

Children's Guide to Insects and Spiders. Jinny Johnson
   (Simon & Schuster)

Eyewitness Explorers: Insects. Steve Parker
   (DK Publishing)

Fascinating World of Ants. Angels Julivert
   (Barrons Educational Series)

Insects First Field Guide. Christina Wilson (Scholastic)

Young Naturalist's Pop-Up Handbook: Beetles.
   Young Naturalist's Pop-Up Handbooks (series).
   Matthew Reinhart (Hyperion)

Web Sites

Ant
www.worldalmanacforkids.com/explore/animals/
   ant.html

Bugbios
www.insects.org

Enchanted Learning
www.zoomschool.com/subjects/insects/ant/

Go to the Ant
home.att.net/~B-P.TRUSCIO/STRANGER.htm

Honey Bee facts
www.honey.com/kids/facts.html

Insecta Inspecta World
www.insecta-inspecta.com

Wonderful World of Insects
www.earthlife.net/insects

Publisher's note to educators and parents: Our editors have carefully reviewed these Web sites to ensure that they are suitable for children. Many Web sites change frequently, however, and we cannot guarantee that a site's future contents will continue to meet our high standards of quality and educational value. Be advised that children should be closely supervised whenever they access the Internet.

Index